AS THEY SAIL

AS THEY SAIL

Samuel Hazo

The University of Arkansas Press
Fayetteville 1999

Other Books by Samuel Hazo

Poetry

The Holy Surprise of Right Now
The Past Won't Stay Behind You
Silence Spoken Here
Nightwords
The Color of Reluctance
Thank a Bored Angel
To Paris
Quartered
Once for the Last Bandit
Twelve Poems
Blood Rights
My Sons in God
Listen with the Eye
The Quiet Wars
Discovery

Fiction

Stills
The Wanton Summer Air
The Very Fall of the Sun
Inscripts

Translations

The Pages of Day and Night
     (Poems of Adonis)
Lebanon: Twenty Poems for One Love
     (Poems of Nadia Tueni)
Transformations of the Lover
The Growl of Deeper Waters
     (Essays of Denis de Rougemont)
The Blood of Adonis

Criticism

Smithereened Apart: A Critique of Hart Crane

Essays

The Pittsburgh That Stays Within You
The Feast of Icarus
The Rest Is Prose
Spying for God

Plays

Feather
Solos
Until I'm Not Here Anymore

Chap Books

Jots Before Sleep
Latching the Fist
Shuffle, Cut and Look

03 02 01 00 99   5 4 3 2 1

Designer: Chiquita Babb

⊗ The paper used in this publication meets the minimum
requirements of the American National Standard for Perma-
nence of Paper for Printed Library Materials Z39.48-1984.

Library of Congress Cataloging-in-Publication Data
Hazo, Samuel John.
    As they sail / Samuel Hazo.
        p.   cm.
    ISBN 1-55728-567-5 (alk. paper)
    I. Title.
    PS3515.A9877A9   1999
    811'.54—dc21   99-28813
                                                CIP

But there isn't a man on earth so proud,
So born to greatness, so bold with his youth,
Grown so brave, or so graced by God,
That he feels no fear as the sails unfurl,
Wondering what fate has willed or will do.

—The Seafarer

When the day comes for my last voyage,
and the ship sails that never returns,
you will find me on board with slim luggage
and almost naked like the sons of the sea.

—Antonio Machado

Acknowledgments

Grateful acknowledgment is made to the *American Scholar, Arts and Letters,* the *Georgia Review, Jusoor,* the *Hudson Review,* the *Laurel Review,* the *Notre Dame Magazine,* the *Notre Dame Review,* the *Pittsburgh Post Gazette,* the *Southern Review, Tar River Poetry,* and the *Texas Observer* in which some of these poems first appeared.

Contents

Just Words   *1*

I. *Born Liars Both*

The Voice of Ernest Hemingway   *5*

Brando   *6*

Gene   *9*

When Nothing's Happening, Everything's Happening   *11*

Ballad of the One-Legged Marine   *13*

Scientia Non Est Virtus   *15*

While Walking on France   *17*

II. *The Speed of Doubt*

Breakdown   *21*

Leafdance   *23*

Cezanne's Atelier near Aix   *25*

Understory   *27*

Innocent Bystanders Are Neither Innocent
 Nor Bystanders   *29*

The Face of Evil in Our Time   *31*

Shall Nothing but Sleep Content You?   *34*

The Lives You Were Born to Live   *36*

When Life Turns Still   *39*

Life Painting   *41*

III. How Satisfaction Differs from Fulfillment

Two Geese on the Killarney Road   45

Every Weekend the Willises Go Away   47

Little (God's) Creature   50

A Parable for Dealing with Your Enemies   52

Bringing the War Home   54

To Be Schooled in Squirrel   55

Ballad of the Jolly Broker   57

IV. No One's Writing This

Jots Before Sleep   61

V. The Earned Wounds of the Road

The Origins of Western Love   79

The Fourteen Happy Days of Abd Al-Rahman III   81

The Egyptian Movie Star   83

Winston   85

The More We Know, the Less We Feel Until   87

The Concise Wisdom of Luggage   89

VI. Just Once in All My Life

A Toast for the Likes of Two   93

Everything's Important, Everything's Brief   96

Max   98

The Thrower and the Keeper   100

To Breathe, to Speak, to Be   102

The First Sam Hazo at the Last   104

Reaching for Australia   106

The Last Shall Be First and Only   108

Ballad of the Old Lovers   110

VII. No Future but the Time at Hand

Dead End   115

American Pastoral   117

A Time of No Shadows   118

Where After This?   120

Arms and the Word   122

Where Were You When?   124

Ahead of Time   125

Just Words

In Arabic a single word
   describes the very act
   of taking a position.
                        Greeks
   pronounce three syllables
   to signify the sense of doom
   that all Greeks fear when things
   are going very well.
                        As for
   the shameful ease we feel
   when bad news happens
   to someone else, including
   friends?
            In Greek—one word.
To designate a hose that funnels
   liquid fire down the turret
   of a tank in battle, the Germans
   speak one word.
                        It's three
   lines long but still one word.
And as for John, Matthew,
   Mark, and Luke?
                        There's not
   a surname in the lot.
                        With just
   one name they match in memory
   the immortality of martyrs.
                        The longer
   they're dead, the more they live . . .

I praise whatever mates
    perception with precision!
                        It asks
    us only to be spare and make
    the most of least.
                    It simplifies
    and lets each word sound final
    as a car door being shut
    but perfect as a telegram to God.

BORN LIARS BOTH

The Voice of Ernest Hemingway

Strange that a man who wrote
  alone so trenchantly
  should be averse to microphones.
His Nobel speech, shorter
  than Faulkner's but as absolute,
  was taped clandestinely by Radio
Havana.
            Hearing it, you catch
  the same electrical staccato
  that opens A *Farewell to Arms*.
He's generous to fellow penmen,
  skeptical of fame and camaraderie
  and what they do to writers
  who pursue them, candid
  in claiming that the best is what's
  not yet been done but cognizant
  of those who tried courageously
  and failed well trying.
                But
  it's the voice, his voice—
  throaty with an almost Spanish
  passion—that can't be unremembered.
For similarity imagine what
  a strong wind does to a high
  flag—the taut fury
  of something staying firmly
  and decisively in place—the poetry
  of utter and intelligent defiance—
  the sinew in the sound—the certainty.

Brando

The best philosophers hate philosophy.
           —Blaise Pascal

You claim what most call love
   is merely a matter of glands
   and genes.
        From one whose mother
   tippled and whose father tupped
   with whores and favored booze and cash,
   that's understandable . . .
              Mistaken
   for a rebel all your life, you've shown
   that you're at home with Shakespeare,
   Toynbee, Augustine, and Kant.
Despite abuse, you've backed—
   in person or with checks—the worthiest
   causes: Indians against
   the government, Jews against
   the Nazis, Palestinians against
   the Irgun Zwei, and hosts of the maligned
   against the merely powerful.
Of all your films you praise
   the one that fewest saw
   and minimize the rest, including
   On the Waterfront (your best).
No star's been imitated more
   by all his peers, but you ignore it
   as you do the Oscars you misplaced
   and scorned.
         If every man's remembered
   for his public self, your legacy

will be the art you somehow
crafted from an industry.
                              Your style
of acting for the camera has no
parallel although you've stressed
that acting is minuscule in your life.
Of course, you're not the first
     to be dismissive of a mastery.
In all things else you say
     you're no more qualified than anyone.
I like your mix of talent,
     spontaneity, tomfoolery, and nerve.
It's made you brazen, unpredictable,
     and blunt.
                    You think Monroe
was killed, but who can say?
You're right about Gable.
                              Gable
     always acted Gable.
                              With due
respect you're only halfway
     right on Bogart.
                         Because
you're always being misinterpreted,
     you keep your counsels to yourself.
When you were young, you
     wrote of loneliness in letter
after letter.
                    Past seventy you live
the loneliness of fame and family
tragedy.
               For peace you've learned
to meditate in California and Tahiti.
If life's a "long climb up

Fool's Hill," you realize there's always
more to know but now
much less to say.
                    The closer
you come to silence, the better.

Gene

No one would raise a presidential no
    against the headlines and the war . . .
Not the "new" Nixon stewing
    in New Jersey, still conniving,
    still the same.
                Not Hubert
Humphrey swilling cow's brains
    near the Pedernales.
                Not Bobby Kennedy.
Not LBJ, the very President . . .
Almost unnoticed, you landed
    in New Hampshire, spoke
    to smallish but determined crowds,
    and entered history.
                Who
    could have guessed your saga
    would include an abdication, murder
    in Los Angeles, a lost election,
    and the Nixon follies?
                All
    for a war that bled on anyway . . .
Later there would be the mockeries.
"Well born or not, he acts
    like a retired auxiliary bishop,
    a monsignor, Saint Achilles
    sulking in his tent."
                Why bother
quoting them?
                Let them discover
who you are in all your poetry

and books.
                    As for the rest,
            it's on the record . . . in the blood . . .
Heroes, of course, make everyone
            uncomfortable.
                    They prod.
                                    They won't
            just go along.
                    They wake us up
            when rather we would sleep.
If only seldom they prevail,
            whoever claimed that heroism
            guarantees salvation in advance?
In airports, dining rooms,
            and public places, people
            understand and quietly salute you
            with their eyes.
                    This shows
            that heroes still define an epoch.
They are what we believe.
                                    They last.

When Nothing's Happening,
Everything's Happening

There's something "old school"
    about you, Charles, and that's
    what I admire most.
                            You still
    believe in friendship, manners,
    duty, generosity, and Launceston.
I've never been to Launceston.
Your postcards proffer me a proper
    Norman town in Cornwall
    topped by a castle.
                            I'm told
    that all your townsmen know
    who Mr. Causley is, and why not?
You schooled three generations there
    for half a century.
                            That keeps
    you dearer to your kin than all
    your books.
                            But it was books
    that paired us for a shared recital
    under Shakespeare's shadow.
                                        After
    Stratford, it was letters, phone
    calls, meeting once in Washington
    and once in Pittsburgh.
                            Now
    it's messages through mutual friends.
Or poetry—especially your dream
    about your parents on a picnic.
Dead for decades, they're sharing tea

and stoppering a milk jug
with a "screw of paper."

                They wave
for you to join them in a feast
that's a reprise of Eden.

                They're young
and happy and in love, and the Cornish
sky shines brighter than the borealis
through your last (and lasting) words . . .
Your letters last as well, and that
includes the jotted postscripts
on the outside flaps.

                It's so damn
good to read what keeps alive
what's dearest to a man.

                It shows
we're not enslaved to memory
or mere presumption—born liars
both.

            It says the present perfect
is the only tense in any tongue,
which means the past is now
whenever poets breathe it
into life again.

            So here's
to the poet from Launceston.

                And here's
to your paper and ink.

                And here's
to the poems borne of your pen
that help us to feel what we think.
So, long live the books that you've written
and long live the books that you'll write
like bread for the dead in the morning
and eyes for the blind at night.

Ballad of the One-Legged Marine

My left leg was gone with the boot still on—
the boot that I laced in the morning.
I felt like a boy who had stepped on a toy
and made it explode without warning.

They choppered me back to a medical shack
with no one but corpsmen to heed me.
I stared at the sky and prayed I would die,
and I cursed when the nurse came to feed me.

I knew that I must, so I tried to adjust
while orderlies struggled to teach me
the will of the crutch and the skill of the cane
and assured me their methods would reach me.

The President came with his generals tame
and explained why he never relieved us.
But the red, white, and blue of my lone right shoe
told the world how he lied and deceived us.

They buried my shin and my bones and my skin
an ocean away from this writing.
But pain finds a way on each given day
to take me straight back to the fighting

when I served with the Corps in a slaughterhouse war
where we tallied our killings like cattle
as if these explain why the armies of Cain
behave as they do in a battle . . .

Whatever's a bore, you can learn to ignore,
but a leg's not a limb you like leaving.
So you deal with regret and attempt to forget
what always is there for the grieving.

If you look for a clue while I stand in a queue,
you can't tell what's real from prosthetic.
I walk with a dip that begins at my hip,
but I keep it discreet and aesthetic.

If you're ordered on line and step on a mine,
you learn what it means to be only
a name on a chart with a hook in your heart
and a life that turns suddenly lonely.

Lose arms, and you're left incomplete and bereft.
Lose legs, and you're fit for a litter.
Lose one at the knee, and you're just like me
with night after night to be bitter.

For Ray Fagan

Scientia Non Est Virtus

The good that I would I do not;
the evil that I would not, that I do.

—Saint Paul

After a week in Paris he saw
　　in a sign a word he'd never
　　learned.
　　　　　Stopping a passerby,
　　he asked in French if he
　　were French.
　　　　　　The response in French
　　could best be rendered as "perhaps . . ."
A month would pass before
　　his laundress asked if many
　　in America wrote poetry.
He told her there were thousands.
"But," she insisted, "do you have
　　one Baudelaire?"
　　　　　　Such anecdotes
　　not only give new meaning
　　to nuance but demonstrate
　　how ignorance differs from knowledge,
　　and knowledge from holy wisdom.
Though ignorance at best means nothing,
　　knowledge may stay the fool of villainy,
　　while villainy plays weevil to the will.
And what's the will except a wayward
　　stallion ridden by our dreams
　　to glory or perdition?
　　　　　　For every
Shakespeare, Lincoln, or Saint Matthew

there's a murderer, liar, reprobate,
or whore who mastered the Brittanica
but stayed the same.
                    Old or young,
we learn too late that being
good is more than strict adherence
to commandments, laws, or codes,
much more than being well
informed, and lightyears more
than all the learning in the world.
What is morality but shunning
    deeds we just can't do even
    when the opportunities present
    themselves?
                    It's reflex
more than choice or reasoning . . .
If that sounds like a substitute
    for ignorance, then ignorance it is.
If it seems paradoxical
    but vaguely possible, it's knowledge.
If it makes sense, it's wisdom.

While Walking on France

Call it the time of bread
   in Cannes: baguettes in stacks
   like ammunition, jumbled croissants,
   and bins of buns and rolls.
At the hotel desk, Sonya
   and Nadeige sing the French
   they speak.
               Madame Antoine,
   whose son Deleuse, Cannonier
   1st Class, died at twenty
   in Algeria, carefully counts coins.
Postcards on the Rue d'Antibes
   remember Gary Cooper, Grace Kelly,
   Bardot, Gabin, and Robert Mitchum.
At the Moulin de Mougins a festival
   ago, Sharon Stone bankrolled
   a banquet for AIDS.
               Villas
   in "high" Cannes nestle (yes,
   like nests) in grottoes guarded
   by monitors and bougainvillea.
                   Bentleys,
   Daimlers, and Porsches cruise
   the Autoroute as privately
   as hearses for the totally enclosed.
Sepulchrally asprawl on beaches
   loll the supine and the prone,
   their tans proceeding by degrees.
Beside a hotel pool a girl
   strips to one triangular swatch

to model swimsuits for the trade . . .
This land where taste is king
   and genuine panache is queen
   attracts and puzzles me.
Does French reluctance spring
   from stubbornness or thought?
What prompts French chocolatiers to make
   the package more seductive than the purchase?
Who but these slim-skulled brothers
   of Rimbaud accord great chefs
   a reverence reserved for kings
   or popes?
                  Each time that France
   is underfoot I memorize
   but never judge why pigeons
   chortle the only song
   they know, how palms upsurge
   into a fountainhead of leaves,
   or why the twin born last
   in France is legally the elder . . .
As men essentialize and women
   existentialize, I focus on ideas
   but ignore the facts.
                        The facts,
   I come to see, are France.
                        They state
   their own philosophy.
                     The more
   I know of it, the less
   I understand.
                  The less I understand,
   the more I know that some
   confusions never yield to reason.

THE SPEED OF DOUBT

Breakdown

Like soldiers ordered to "Fall in,"
   platoons of starlings swoop
   and muster on a telephone line.
Equidistant and at perched attention,
   they mimic ranks at "Parade rest."
Suddenly they dive into the air
   on cue, swirling in a bluster
   of wings like a dream gone mad.
For just that long, I think
   that madness rules the world,
   despite appearances.
                       "Change
   the rhythm," Pindar predicted,
   "and the walls of the city will fall."
It takes so little . . .
                 Vary
   the height and width of stairs
   by just a fraction, and the rhythm
   of a stairway dies.
               Alter
   traffic patterns, and we slacken
   to the speed of doubt.
               Or let
come war, and we're undone
as if the sea breathed in
and never out against our shores,
surrounding, pounding, drowning
everything.
            It imitates what happens
when I'm writing, and the words

won't perch.
               They swirl berserk
like panicked flocks in flight.
They're swirling now.
                   I'm losing
touch with what I should be saying,
and I can't remember what I think
I meant.
            The tempo's totally
undone . . .
               Pindar was right.

Leafdance

The more I rake, the more
   they come.
            The flutterers.
                  The dry
   engulfers.
         Those that waft
   like wings in the wind.
               The lithe
   cartwheelers and the circling hordes.
Unstoppable the lot of them
   after their slow, chromatic dying . . .
Sailplanes.
         Helicopters.
                  Parachutists.
Skitterers.
         Divers and dawdlers.
Blusters of frayed flags
   that whistle from the highest branch,
   the brittle, the burnt by the cold,
   the starfish and the crumpling moth . . .
Rake them, rake every single one.
From such a harvest comes
   at last so little . . .
               Rake
   while you're able, rake and put
   them to the match.
               And let
   their steady crackling make an ash
   of sickles, scythes, and all

that puts an end to anything
before it's due.
                    Or ready.

Cezanne's Atelier near Aix

It's as he left it, or as it
    left him after he painted it.
A sprawl of dappled quince,
    three pipes, and two pairs
    of spectacles command a tabletop.
A crumpled tam relaxes
    at the opposite end.
                        I think
    a lamp centers the two,
    but I could be wrong.
                        Recently
    an opthomologist appraised
    the spectacles and saw how fuzzy
    and miscolored they made everything
    appear.
                He wondered if Cezanne's
    whole alphabet of color
    erred as a result.
                        Call it
    impressionism or call it
    a mistake, but Sainte-Victoire
    seems falsely brown beside
    the real thing.
                        It's reminiscent
    of El Greco, isn't it?
                        His portraiture
    of Christ and saints and bishops
    with their equine faces, upturned
    eyes, and lengthened bodies
    wasn't Gothic, as the critics claim.

El Greco's optic flaw turned
   circles into ovals, ovals
   into candleflames, and horizontals
   somehow into verticals.
                              Like Paul
   Cezanne he painted what he saw
   though all he saw was wrong.
Astigmatism was his problem, not
   perspective.
                        If what resulted
   was majestic, how do you explain it?
Does art transcend man's failings?
Do masterpieces simply happen?
Should art historians be qualified
   in opthomology?
                     If you regard
   such questions as redundant
   or ridiculous, then you explain
   El Greco.
                  You explain Cezanne.

Understory

It's not that sometimes I forget.
I'm told that everybody does.
What troubles me is how
    whatever I've forgotten trebles
    in importance the more I keep
    forgetting it.
            Some word . . .
                    Some place . . .
Today a student from the Class
    of Way Back When
    seemed certain I'd remember him
    by name.
          I tried and tried
    before I had to ask . . .
                  Though students
    and ex-students are my life,
I must admit that I remember
most of the best, all
of the worst, many who have left
this world, and not that many
of the rest.
           It leaves me wondering . . .
Is memory a beast that sheds
    its baggage as it goes?
Are facts by definition destined
    for oblivion?
          Or is it absolute
    that what I can't forget no matter
    how I try is all that's worth
    remembering?

I know a mother
of four sons who mixes up
their names.
                    Ollie is Bennett.
Bennett is Drew.
                    Drew
is Christopher.
                    Facing one,
she travels down the list before
she pleads, "Tell me your name,
dear boy."
                    Outsiders realize
they're all one boy to her,
regardless of their names.
                              She knows
them by their souls.
                              That reassures me.

For JoAnn Bevilacqua-Weiss

Innocent Bystanders Are Neither Innocent Nor Bystanders

QUESTION: *What is the most dangerous profession in the world today?*
ANSWER: *Innocent bystander.*

It's easy to talk when the creek's
   a trickle or just a meandering
   fuse of slime between dry rocks.
But what will you say when the creek's
   a stream, and the stream's in flood,
   and the flood's upon you?
                       What
will you do?
                Angry brown
water's as deaf as falling
bombs or charging bulls.
If you are spared, you'll wonder
   why you happened to be standing
   in the way.
             Why you?
                  Why there?
But then why not?
             Later
   you'll do what most survivors do —
   live recklessly, live all
   you can, live till it hurts.
In time the hurt will be enough
   to make you think.
                You'll cultivate
   an interest in biography.
                You'll read
   about those kings who, facing death,

insisted that their tea be brewed
henceforth from women's tears.
You'll learn how frail Sir Antony
dined morning, night, and noon
on lobster tails until the last.
You'll be intrigued but unimpressed.
To feel much less alone
you'll travel to decountrify yourself,
confide in sympathetic strangers,
and return to what's no longer
quite the same as home.
                            You'll turn
from one diversion to another,
and they'll never seem to end.
But somehow they will help you
 in the way a mirror curved
behind a bar convinces solitary
drinkers that they have at least
and still and finally one friend.

The Face of Evil in Our Time

> *. . . the banality of evil . . .*
>
> —Hannah Arendt

> *The Devil's cleverest wile is to convince us that he does not exist.*
>
> —Charles Baudelaire

Passport-photo plain: Dillinger
   in golfer's slacks, Landru
   relaxing like the altar boy
   he was, Stalin of the "Uncle Joe"
   mustache with Edgeworth pipe
   tobacco glowing in his calabash,
   Hitler summering in Berchtesgaden.
No fangs, no madman's drool,
   scarcely a sneer.
               They look
   as common as the rest of us.
Yet Dillinger killed men for sport.
Landru, who poisoned and reduced
   to ash more women than the court
   could number, doodled his trial
   away and smiled in the guillotiner's
   face.
         Killing his country's
   match of Sweden's total
   census was Stalin's way
   of keeping Russia leninized.
And Hitler's legacy needs only
   to be known to horrify again.
Of the aforementioned who looks

the least suspicious or the most
innocuous?
                Possibly all four . . .
Who said that crimes and criminals
  must rhyme?
                  Manson and his kind
  have poisoned us with melodramatized
  debauch, satanic symbols,
  blood on the ceiling.
                    Whether
  they kill just once or seriatim,
  we like our murderers depraved.
As usual, we're wrong.
                  Real evil
  at its worst does not declare
  itself.
          It cowers like the smallest
  of the smallest cancers on a slide,
  happy if it's never seen
  or else mistakenly identified.
Basic humanity and the inability
  to live with guilt prevent
  the basest criminals from saying
  what they did.
                  So jails are filled
  with innocent men who plead
  the sweet hypocrisy of looking
  nondescript or temporarily insane.
Likewise, the lawful hell called war
  seems absolutely interchangeable
  with murder in cold blood.
My-Lai, where villagers
  were "wasted but not killed,"
  made murder murderless.

                    And what
of all those Filipino nurses
in Chicago strangled one
by one five decades back?
The strangler was a handyman named
    Speck.
            Condemned without parole,
he fattened unremorsefully in prison
and enjoyed his sentence.
                    Speck
was his Christian name . . .
                        Speck.

Shall Nothing but Sleep Content You?

Approaching age, you wake
   at night for the usual reasons.
Until you learned the nonchalance
   of furniture, this bothered you.
In French the word for furniture
   translates as moveables.
                At night
   these moveables command a house.
By touch they tell you where
   you are.
          They teach you to forget
   that Shakespeare wrote: "The night
   is long that never finds the day."
They help you understand why pharoahs
   feared the dark and praised
   the sun with pyramids.
              At once
   in motion though at rest, they are
   what everybody does and is.
By day, the work.
           By night,
   the weariness . . .
            You learn from this.
Learn what?
         Whatever occurs to you . . .
That only the twice seen
   is truly seen, which is the why
   of memory and all the arts . . .
That life is nine-tenths chance
   and one-tenth choice, which makes

acceptance truer than anticipation . . .
That satisfaction is the bread of death,
   which means that matching life
   with appetite makes life its own
   worst enemy . . .
                    Your audience of moveables
   approves these throwaways.
                           Or so
you think . . .
               But company is company,
and you accept their mute applause
like salutations from the deaf.
                      What
are these after all but throwaways
themselves?
             Predestined for the fire
sale and finally the fire,
they prevail as briefly as your thoughts.
But still their presences console,
   console, console . . .
                 You think
of homeless men alone tonight
and blanketed by cardboard over
subway grates.
              No moveables for them . . .
Awake and cold, what wouldn't
   they offer for the least of these?

The Lives You Were Born to Live

Don't tell your doctor that you're
    waking up at 3:00 A.M.,
    forgetting what you're just about
    to mention, nodding off for no
    reason, feeling the noose tighten
    year by year.
                        He'll tell you,
    "Symptoms of narcolepsy—common
    and incurable."
                        Or else, "I guess
    we're headed for 'assisted living'
    sooner than we think."
                                It does
    no good to claim that life's
    the art of dying in your skin
    as if you're not or that
    the life your living's not
    the life you planned.
                        So,
    why blame kidneys if they keep
    Pacific Time?
                        Or fault the ships
    of memory that jettison their cargoes
    as they sail?
                        And as for years . . .
When were they never blind
    as justice and as ultimate?
                                Regardless,
    there are no birthdays for the soul.

It is and is and is
    and is and is.
                    It gives
improbability the time it needs
to happen by surprise.
                    It lets
the unpredictable become our lives
as certainly as geneology
no matter how we mutter
or philosophize . . .
                    I know
a widower who sold his holdings
for a long-term billet
of assisted living.
                    Once there,
he met a widow who had done
the same.
                    Without intending it
they fell in love, then left
the premises with promises to live
assisted only by each other.
Later they wondered why
    they wasted all those years
    preparing carefully and safely
    to be dead.
                    Of course, they're waiting
still, but now they're spared the fate
of being obselete, ignored, passé.
Some days they can't contain
    the happiness they feel they don't
    deserve.
                    They fear for one
another more than for themselves.

They wonder who will be the first
to die and who'll be left alone.
And when?
            And how?
                        And why?

When Life Turns Still

For years I never understood
   why painters painted so complete
   a contradiction.
                   If down and up
   were opposites by definition,
   then stillness and life could not
   be more at odds.
               But how
   explain away Cezanne,
   who posed in absolute perfection
   all those apples, grapes, carafes,
   and cheeses on a tray—one blink
   of ripeness just before the rot?
Was every still life for Cezanne
   like music to Stravinsky—not horizontal
   melody but vertical sounds
   in sequence heard in separation,
   each one a song unto itself
   like ranks in a parade?
               Stravinsky's
   theory was to make us listen up
   instead of listen on.
              And that
made sense.
            If life could end
   at any moment, every moment
   was eternal and unique.
              Ergo,
Cezanne.
        Ergo, Stravinsky.

Stillness and verticality versus
  motion and protraction . . .
Last night I saw a woman
  in her sixties whom I dated
  when she turned nineteen.
         I still
  remember how she curled against
  my shoulder when we danced—
  the scent of lily in her hair,
  the oval of her waist.
        Seeing
  how time had made a raisin
  of her face, I understood the sacred
  once of everything and how
  the truthful lies of art
  seem truer than our passing lives.
Is it so wrong to show impossibility
  the factual defiance of a dream?
To say what was still is
  because it was?
       To lead us
  grudgingly through silence
  into gratitude?
      Let us
  keep still.
     Let us be grateful.

Life Painting

Three days of laundry wait
    for her at home.
                    Her neck
    is stiff from posing.
                    Twice
minimum wage is what she's earning,
    and the class is mixed.
                    Her nipples
    harden in the cold.
                    She itches
    where she'd never scratch herself
    in public.
                    She tries to think
    about the wash and how abundantly
    the sheets will billow in the dryer . . .
Females behind their easels
    see her merely as another
    of their kind, observing where
    she's fat and where she's not.
They sketch her face with more
    attention than they give the rest
    of her.
                    The men see more—
a woman nakedly employed—
twin dimples in her lower
back—the vortex in the loins
    where all desires end,
    and life's set free.
                    Desire's
    in the air.

The men pay less
attention to the woman's face
than to her thighs.
Someone
announces that the sitting's over.
The painters pack their tubes
and brushes.
Seen from above
the class might seem a tight
isosceles of billiard balls
transformed from nouns to verbs
precisely when the cue ball
strikes.
They scatter to their lives.
The model reaches for her robe.
She scans each drying canvas
as she leaves.
Not one resembles her.

HOW SATISFACTION DIFFERS FROM FULFILLMENT

Two Geese on the Killarney Road

They waddled as the Dutch once tromped
   abreast in wooden sandals,
   and our bus be damned.
                We turned
   into their audience.
            They kept
   in step like fat, flat-footed,
   and accredited ambassadors to courts
   no longer on the map.
           For all
   they cared we might as well
   have stayed in Dublin or America.
Earlier we'd waited for a clan
   of Holsteins to surrender half
   the road.
          We trailed their swaying
   udders past Tralee before
   the driver gently fired
   his horn.
         The herd divided
   into shores and let us through
   like Moses all the way to Dingle.
Later it was mares — or rather
   one stray mare that needed
   only to be shown how easily
   the fallen fence that set her free
   would let her back again.
I leave to your imagination how
   we fared with lambs and one
   quick fox.

They watched us
warily as creatures watch
intruders who might yet be friends.
They felt our presence say
the world was ours.
In goose
or cow or horse or lamb
or fox they answered, "What's
the fuss?
Don't push.
Don't honk.
Don't rush.
The earth is free
and public as the sky.
There's room
for you.
There's room for us."

Every Weekend the Willises Go Away

Fingering her breasts for trouble,
   she hears him say, "I've yet
   to find out who I am."
                      "You're
Willis Willis, husband mine,
   and I'm your lawful, bedded wife."
"Is Phyllis Willis all you really are?"
"The rhyme's a bummer, but at least
   we match."
              Without another word
   he dons his rainbow Rebok
   running shoes and jogs his daily
   dozen miles alone.
                Later
   when she gives herself to him,
   she keeps on chewing popcorn
   on her knees and tells him to be quick.
Next day, leaving the Pekinese
   to sit the house, they pack
   the Jeep and head for the mountains.
"For me, home's always up ahead,"
   he says as he steers. "Go,
   go, go—that's life."
                 "Really?
I thought that life's what happens
   when you stay at home."
                 She thinks
   about her guestroom with no
   guests, the stacks of China
   she has never used, the silver

service tarnishing in cellophane.
She thinks about the Pekinese
    asleep on a cushion, surrounded
    by silence . . .
                    The cabin greets them
    as they left it: an inch of last
    week's Pepsi in a paper cup,
    the toilet-water filmed with ice
    like paraffin but flushable, the telephone
    he keeps refusing to connect.
"What happens, Will, if we need help—
    a helicopter, Medivac?"
                            "The tough
    get going when the going gets
    tough.
            Dick Nixon did it—
    so can we."
                    That night
    they sleep like campers in their jeans.
She wakes at seven, sidles
    to the shower, and slips on a tile.
Her ankle cracks like a twig
    in a bonfire.
                    Two hundred
    Jeep-miles later she's in pain
    and plaster of Paris.
                    "Just tough
    it out," he tells her when he leaves,
    "and we can still do Mexico
    by June or maybe Argentina—
    go, go, go."
                    His words keep
    fading like a voice beyond the grave.

Nothing he tells her matters
     anymore.
               She wonders who
     this stranger is and how
     they came to meet and why
     she ever let him in her body.
The plastic bracelet on her wrist
     reminds her of a handcuff.
She wants so much to sleep
     like Snow White with a broken ankle
     long enough to waken healed and changed
     somewhere she's never been
     as someone else—with someone else.

Little (God's) Creature

Do you want to know what love is? Get a dog.
—Mona Van Duyn

Simply by lying down and being
　　dog, he demonstrates how
　　satisfaction differs from fulfillment.
Oscar's fulfilled.
　　　　　　　　Without
　　a clock he knows the time
　　of night, of year, of age.
So far his only fears are horses,
　　storms, and any fellow dog
　　too large or amorous for comfort.
A miniature horse, he prances
　　to his meals, eschewing dogchow
　　totally unless disguised.
In cars he rides shotgun—
　　head periscoping out the window,
　　ears sleeked and flattened
　　by the wind, eyes orientaled
　　into squints and taking aim.
What makes me love this pooch
　　who weighs no more than both
　　my shoes?
　　　　　　　Is it his absolute
　　defiance when he fights?
　　　　　　　　　　Is it
　　because he pays attention
　　and accepts contentment as life's
　　best reward?
　　　　　　　Is it because

he thinks precisely with his nose
and chats concisely with his tail?
Or is it just his irreplaceability?
Each night he lies beside me
    while I read.
                In dog's arithmetic
    he's half my age, but catching up . . .
How innocent he is of malice,
    treachery, impatience, envy,
    and the fear of death.
                    I read.
He sleeps.
        We share mortality
    in silence, breath by breath.

A Parable for Dealing with Your Enemies

Imagine you have all the coins
    of all the currencies on earth.
Strangers start asking you
    for change.
                They hand you bills
of such denominations as to seem
beyond arithmetic.
                Each time
you finish one transaction
you must face another.
                Everybody
smiles and smiles as you count
and double-check in all the languages
you know.
                You're steadily
reduced to speaking numbers,
nothing else.
                That you speak
history and poetry and politics
is totally irrelevant.
                Your
customers are not concerned
with anything except to keep you
occupied with what they want.
They form a queue that reaches
    the horizon.
                You see that you'll be
making change for strangers
day by day from now
until the day you die.

Then
and only then do you rebel.
You say you're out to lunch
forever.
They claim your only
duty is to give them change
whenever they demand it.
Each time
you answer what they ask,
they ask you something else
or something more.
You keep
your poise no matter what
they call you, and they call you
everything.
You speak in verbs
and nouns and pauses now,
not numbers anymore.
They swear
you'll hear from them or from
their lawyers over this.
You keep on talking, sometimes
in language, sometimes in silence.
You don't need their money.

Bringing the War Home

The groundhog stood supreme
    as Churchill in our yard.
                        He held
    his ground to prove his predecessors
    owned this hill for years
    before the invention of real
    estate.
             Between us flowed
    a channel of grass.
                 His attitude
    reminded me of Churchill's sculpture
    in the wings of Parliament—defiant,
    squat, woodchuckian . . .
                     Churchillian
    or not, the mood was sure
    to vanish if I stirred or spoke.
The woods would take him back.
The grass would turn into a lawn
    again.
            But not before
    he'd made a stance of it,
    this burrower.
               By staying put
    he made me think he'd fight
    to death and never flee
    with right on the side of him
    and might on the side of me.

To Be Schooled in Squirrel

1

Nothing moves exactly
  like a squirrel.
             Not even
  another squirrel.
             Not even
  the same squirrel in a different
tree.
    Or a different squirrel
  in the same tree.
            Or the same
  squirrel in the same tree.

2

Nothing's direct.
          Each day
  you'll zigzag like a squirrel
  that hugs its way spread-eagled
  and a-stutter up a maple
  trunk.
     The feat will be
  to climb and cling until
  you finally run out of tree.
In retrospect the climb will be
  what matters—just the climb.
Sometimes you'll change
  from climbing to descending
  a la squirrel.
         Hugging the trunk

for life itself you'll hang there
upside down.
                Nothing will look
the same.
            You'll understand
a bat's inverted panorama—
the view that Peter had
of Rome when he was crucified
head downward on the Palatine—
the mystery of Fred Astaire
tapdancing with his cane
across a ceiling.
               Everything
will say it's new, it's new.
It's just a matter of position.

Ballad of the Jolly Broker

Nothing was surer amid all the furor
than watching a stock that I picked on a hunch
make rich men of paupers, and paupers of fools,
and all in the pinch that it took to eat lunch.

My betting and cheering took real engineering.
I guessed and I gauged and I bet and I prayed
from the dawn of the bull to the dusk of the bear
where fortunes were waiting and fortunes were made.

The world of percents is a world that resents
whenever its buyouts are less than a steal.
Its language is numbers, and numbers are lethal,
and all that makes sense is the luck of the deal.

You have to like poker to be a good broker.
You have to take chances and hope for the best.
Buy cheap and sell dear is the law of the market,
and woe unto those who forget or protest.

Like any good broker I loved to play poker,
but poker's a gamble where all that you've got
is the lure of the cards and the stack of the chips
and the dice of the draw and the pay of the pot . . .

I took all my winnings that some called my sinnings
and lived like a king where the snow never fell.
I drank all my juices and swallowed my pills
and bet on the races, and down came hell . . .

It cost me my wife in the prime of my life.
It made me content with much less than the best.
I worked for the day when I never would work,
and the money was sure, and the honey was rest.

If you'd rather be healthy than feeble and wealthy . . .
If you'd rather be happy than wed to a bed,
then think of a man with a millionaire's tan
who died half a lifetime before he was dead.

NO ONE'S WRITING THIS

Jots Before Sleep

We share a world when we are awake;
each sleeper is in a world of his own.

—Heraklitos

1

Bare but for pajamas, I'm dressed
    for the occasion.
                    Or am I underdressed?
Regardless, I board the bed
    and wait for the waiting third
    of this and all my days
    to overtake me.
               Two-thirds
    vertical, one-third horizontal—
    that's the ratio.
             I wait
    for sleep to swallow me
    exactly as the ocean swallows
    a body—totally and without mercy.
Silent, without scent or gravity,
    my dreams will imitate Utrillo's paintings
    or the photos of Atget—vistas
    without a soul in sight.
The murderers who've yet to strike
    are hiding there—diseases,
    warfare, crime, malevolence,
    revenge, and accident.
               They're poised
    like eagles on a peak who scan
    for prey before they blink
    and dive into the air.

                        There's no
defense.
                Tomorrow I'll awaken
like a man spared, knowing
I'm exempt no more, just lucky,
that all still left alive are lucky.
I think of what Sofia said,
    "My mother prayed for a good death,
    that's all, and she and my father
    died alike—no suffering, no comas—,
    they just died."
                        To keep from drowning
in a dream, I play the writer's game—
trying to say shortly what's long
or longly what's too short . . .
It's Norfolk—forty years ago . . .
Rainfall makes a torrent of the road.
A terrier decides to cross
    before my Chevrolet.
                        It's swerve
or hit the terrier.
                        I swerve.
No one's approaching in the left-hand
    lane.
            If so, I'm long since dead,
and no one's writing this.

    2

Ebony, with yellow oriental eyes,
    the panther paces on his paws
    behind his bars.
                        Three paces
    left, three paces right,

three paces left, three paces
right . . .
           The pacing mimics
music from a scratched record
when the needle sticks.
                The panther
paces in his prison like a murderer
in solitary.
           Killing's in his eyes,
his growl, his stalker's muscles
tight as knots beneath his pelt.

3

The Arabs believe that haste
   is a sign of bad breeding . . .
The women of Africa wear
   decorative hats and colorful
   scarves and flowers in their hair
   in sacred tribute to the head . . .
The Latins measure the worth
   of a political leader by his skill
   in oratory, the size of his entourage,
   and how long his audience
   will wait to hear him speak . . .

4

"Now here's a politician says
   he knows the mind of South
   America," he muttered as he sat.
   "How's that for modesty?"
                She had
the look of someone studying

her favorite piece of jewelry
alone.

He crunched the pages
of the paper like excelsior.

"Ads,
ads, ads—you need a microscope
to find the news."

She smiled
and asked, "Do you remember
what happened thirty years
ago today?"

"The Yankees won
the pennant?"

"No."

"Armstrong
claimed the moon for Nixon?"

"No."

"I bought that clinker
of an Oldsmobile?"

"You asked me
to marry you."

"And what was your answer?"

"I refused."

"Why?"

"Cary Grant
asked me first."

"What made you
change your mind about him?"

"You."

"Me?"

Just then
she noticed it—the small white
box no larger than a domino

beside the telephone.
                            "What's
in the box?"
                    "Maybe it's something
from Cary Grant."
                            After opening
the velvetine lid, she plucked
the ring and eased her finger
into it.
            She posed.
                        He focused
on the team standings in the National
League West.
                    She let the ring
bewitch her as she modeled it
and hummed.
                    "Cary?"
                            "Yes."
"You'll have to help me take
    this off."
                "I'll try," he said
and reached for the ring.
                            "Not that,"
she said, guiding his hand
to the belt of her robe, " . . . this."

    5

"What's sex," she asked, "without love?"
"What's love," he said, "without sex?"
Such words were certain to perplex
    with him beneath and her above.

6

It promises to be a heaven
   of precision: fortunes computed
   to the decimal, thermometers and clocks
   in digital, all history compacted
   on a chip with nothing left
   to mystery.
              Each citizen will be
   in lightning touch with anybody
   anywhere on earth but intimate
   with none, including himself.
                     Out
   of the loop will be all those
   who claim the privilege of error
   and unguaranteed results.
                 Poets
   will be told that poetry does not
   compute.
             Actors and artists
   will be deemed irrelevant but useful
   as decor or atmosphere.
               The news
   will be a nightly list with videos
   of murders, rapes, assassinations,
   fires, crashes, thefts,
   and floods parenthesized by baseball
   scores and weather bytes.
               Each year
   we'll gather at a point called X
   and tell each other via Internet
   how lucky and informed we are.

7

After sixty, why quibble?
Women drip, and men dribble.

8

Like a climber lost in a squall,
    the old man proffers me
    a ring of keys—lock keys,
    door keys, car keys, cornucopias
    of keys.
                He offers them like gifts.
He wants to know which opens what.

9

On a televised show from a zoo,
    the tiniest cub, Bartholomew,
    meows his squeal into a growl.
He claws a ball of yarn
    before he settles in cat-sleep,
    his paws and knuckles soft
    as pillows pillowing his jaws . . .
Somewhere in Africa his counterparts
    are imitating him—teasing
    like kittens, suckling in pairs,
    or sprawled on one another
    for a group snooze.
                    The lioness
looks bored.
                    The balding or younger
    males are sleeping off a kill—
    their mop-tipped tails at work
    on flies, their ears atwitch

when a butterfly lands.

                    Earlier,
a pride of five had trapped
a water buffalo and clawed it
to its knees, its entrails spilling
as it fell.

          The lioness watched
and licked her cubs.

                    Later,
she would hunt at night, alone.

10

It was the most leisurely snowfall I'd ever seen—
not the kind of snow where the descending
flakes flutter and slant as if unsure of where
they ought to land. Or if they should. These
flakes were small as rain but infinitely lighter.
Like paper ashes in slow motion they sifted down
by the tens of thousands with all the flakes
exactly the same distance from one another.

11

Who needs to be acknowledged?
Poems are their own acknowledgment.
Simply by happening, they praise
    the poets who created them.
Tortuous as love and just
    as jealous, poetry's price
    is absolute attention on demand.
It shadows those it claims
    the way a killer's shadow
    shadows a killer to his killing

and beyond.
                    Small wonder
few endure.
                    One life's
too brief, one world's too small
for words it takes a world
of lifetimes to acknowledge
on a page.
                    Robinson Jeffers,
that Pittsburgh Protestant turned
California prophet, understood.
In poems darker than Hardy's
    he scorned what lesser men revered.
Choosing boulders the Pacific
    bowled ashore, he hefted them
    to higher ground and wedged them
    into walls until the walls became
a house.
                    The best intentioned
offers of assistance he refused.
He built alone exactly
    as he wrote alone and died
    at last within that very house
alone.
                    Raise Jeffers
from the dead and ask if ever
he depended on acknowledgment
or praise.
                    He'd laugh in your face.

12

                    Poetry's said,
                    prose read.

13

Sidling up behind her, Eric cooed,
   "Your legs are so distinctive
   I can spot them even from the back."
Expecting his wife to turn
   around, he gasped when a woman
   he had never seen confronted him.
"I'm sorry . . ." he began.

                 She smacked him
   with her purse across his cheek
   so hard he lost a filling . . .
Wearing her white strapless
   for the first and final time,
   Rebecca climbed the ballroom
   stairs.

       Someone behind her
   stepped on her hem and stayed there.
Rebecca kept on climbing . . .
Anxious to shave after landing
   at La Guardia, Fred lathered
   and faced the restroom mirror.
He finished one cheek when two
   women entered, gasped,
   and left.

       Another woman
   came and screamed.

               An airport
   guard came last and asked
   as Fred re-shouldered his suspenders,
   "Sir, do you realize just where
   you are?"

       No matter what he said,
   it sounded unconvincing.

                    What
was the aftermath?
                    Eric delivered
    all his compliments thereafter
    face to face in private.
Rebecca realized that shame,
    compared to guilt, was temporary.
And Fred was warned that separate
    but equal meant exactly
    what it said with violators risking
    fines or imprisonment or both.

    14

It's time we walked.
                    Not
    with the stomp of a sergeant-at-arms,
    the double-timing cadences
    of drummers on parade, the slant
    of waiters shouldering trays
    of gumbo in saucered bowls,
    the shuffle of captives in chains.
Never the goosestep, the swagger
    of braggarts, the scissoring strut
    of matriarchs empowered
    by their daggering, hammering heels,
    and absolutely not the rush
    of passengers in helter-panic
    dashing for connecting flights.
Rather a slow meander
    in feathering snow, a stroll
    without a destination or a purpose,
    the saunter of athletic dancers

after their best performances,
the near loiter of browsers
or the amble of one who walks
an inquisitive dog.
                    Rather
anything that slackens us
to match the heart's unstoppable,
precise, and permanent insurgency —
no slower, no faster than that.

15

At first they soar like Piper
     Cubs until they flex their wings,
     and suddenly they're hawks — two hawks
     on high she's watching as she sips
     black coffee from a mug
     that's saucered on a headline
     bannering in capital letters
     a crash in Pennsylvania.
                         The hawks
perform a *pas de deux*,
and she forgets for half a second
all the passengers destroyed in Hopewell
when the jet went down.
                         That memory
will shadow her tomorrow like a dog
she'll never lose.
                    The hawks
are her salvation.
                    They sail and swing
     like dancers in a Balanchine ballet.
She lets her coffee steam.
                         Her soul

is with the hawks.
                              She has
the look she'd have if she
were dancing with Nijinsky in a dream.

16

Sometimes I leave the house
    without a dime on purpose.
The air tastes sweeter then
    because I'm thinking as I breathe.
I watch the callow lilies aim
    untaxable yellow bugles
    at the sun while penniless sparrows
    joust for a priceless crust.
Flat broke, I'm worth the same
    as these — worth more because
    I've chosen worthlessness.
                              This keeps
    me intimate with all I see
    the way that sharing secrets
    makes the sharers intimate.
                              What
    difference does it make if fools
    believe that decimals and ammunition
    rule the world?
                    Who cares
    for decimals and ammunition?
                              Waiving
    the price of admission, I can count
    a convoy of clouds in passage
    to New Jersey.
                    The mint's
    on fire with green.

The elms
are slender and symmetrical
as chalices.
          A chipmunk scrams
to his nest, and the clouds fly on.
There's never an intermission.

17

When I'm with those who start
all conversations with conclusions,
I realize the conversation's over.
Others incapable of error
or apology reduce me to a shrug
unless I lose my temper.
                    Gossips
confirm that gossip shrinks
the gossiper . . .
          If life's an unrehearsed
and unrehearsable play in which
we're cast without auditions,
what good is disquisition, blab,
or mere retort?
          Better to know
we need each other as we need
the air.
          Better the open air
than shriveling in graves we fit
while we're alive.
          Each day
they bury us before we're dead
when all we want is just
to be forgiven and forgive.
                    Not seven

but seventy times seven times
is how God tells us
   to forgive.
            Shall God do less?
Can God in fact do less?
If not, then I say now
   to hell with hell.
                  The gift
of gifts is mercy.
                  What threatens us
with fire or with fear is frivolous.

THE EARNED WOUNDS
OF THE ROAD

The Origins of Western Love

The Arabs of Andalús bequeathed
   the troubadours a minstrelsy
   where love and passion sang.
Latins ignored the song.
Gaius Valerius Catullus
   and his tribe preferred coupling
   on impulse and praising it in couplets
afterward.
             The mix created
courtly love.
             From courtly love
came all the legends of romance,
and from romance the dream where love
of passion seemed more impassioned
than the passion of love.
             Still, we must
be fair.
          Though wiving and wenching
gave way to wiving or wenching,
a few still lived the passionate
friendship that is marriage.
             But
most remained as permanently
parallel as railroad tracks
that never meet except
at the horizon.
          And even there
it's an illusion.
          No wonder
choosing one another every

day became a chore while coupling
on the sly assumed the guise
of ecstasy.
                    But why be righteous?
We're lovers all, and love
without responsibility is every lover's
dream of happiness.
                         Yet all
that lasts is not what prompts
but what survives the act.
                              If man's
a wallet waiting to be spent,
the question's never whether
but with whom.
                    And why.
                              If woman
is a purse whose body's mouths
are drawstrung shut until
she gives herself away,
the question's never whether
but with whom.
                    And why.
                         The Arabs
thought the why unsayable and sang
the beauties of the where and when.
Catullus settled for the how.
Both felt they sang the answer then
to something unexplainable
before.
          Or since.
                    Or now.

The Fourteen Happy Days of Abd Al-Rahman III

I have known only fourteen happy days in my life.
—Last words of Abd Al-Rahman III

The first was when he heard
   her name: Azahara.
                The second
was the time he met her
and decided that the caliphate
would be an empty throne
without her.
                The third was when
he married her.
                The fourth
was how she came to him
without her veils.
                He touched
her nipples like the very grapes
of God, loosened her hair,
and later felt her inner
thighs against his flanks
like the soft, strong wings
of a swan.
                The fifth was the son
she gave him.
                The sixth
he never revealed.
                The seventh
was the year he liberated Andalús
and Córdoba.
                The eighth was when
the palace at Medina was completed

as his gift to her.
                    The ninth
was how she smiled when he named
the glories of the palace: 4,000
columns, 13,700 servants
plus 3,500 pages, eunuchs,
and slaves to crumble 1,000 loaves
a day for the palace fish.
The tenth was when he chose
to rule in rags and smear
himself with sand to conquer
vanity.
          The eleventh he never
revealed.
            The twelfth was when
she died, holding his each
hand and speaking as her final
word his name.
                  The thirteenth
he never revealed.
                    The fourteenth
was the day he welcomed death
because it meant he'd never
have to bear the agony
of one more day without her.

The Egyptian Movie Star

In Arabic her name meant splendor,
  and splendorously she walked in lavender
  from scarf to shoe.
                      Her lips
  relaxed into a practiced smile.
Her hips did all the talking
  as she strolled like Nefertiti
  to the Chardonnay and shrimp.
                          Standing,
  she seemed to move.
                      Moving,
  she stood in motion.
                      She said
  her gate to paradise was Hollywood,
  not Mecca.
                Sharif the Lebanese
  had made it in disguise.
                          Why couldn't
  a bonafide Cairene?
                    Splendor
  and Brando on a shared marquee . . .
Splendor's each handprint
  in cement . . .
                  Splendor encircled
  by photographers . . .
                      For emphasis
  she crossed her arms beneath
  her breasts to give them lift
  and forward outwardness.

Later
she crossed them differently
to give them outward forwardness.
And so she ripened like an orchid
waiting to be picked, her lashes
inked with kohl, her earrings
shimmering like tiny chandeliers,
her Cleopatra bracelets by the dozen
adding splendor on splendor to Splendor.

Winston

"Pink seashells—they easy,
    they in the shallow water,
    but the brown ones, they deep,
    they for the best divers,
    like me, Winston."
                            His gold
    bicuspid glints like a ring
    when he grins.
                        Between us
    gleam shells like armadillos
    or rainbow tornadoes of bone.
"I dive myself for all these
    shell.
                    I wash them every one
    myself.
                        I dive.
                                    I sell.
You want good shell, see Winston."
One size too tight, his shirt
    front screams at the buttonholes.
When he squats, his underwear
    droops through a slit in the seam
    of his shorts scissored from old
    trousers at the knees . . .
                                    I see him
    younger by twenty years,
    a boy after his first dive,
    hawking starfish and grinning ivory.
Then, twenty years ahead,
    too old to dive, toothless,

selling green sunhats
woven from belts of palm.
Only that gold biter will not stop
glistening like wealth itself
amid this paradise of tourists, orchids,
shanties, and the slopping undertow
that swills the beach like mop water.

The More We Know, the Less We Feel Until

Down from her waist, she rolled
   her white bikini bottom
   like a wee inverted sock.
Sunned evenly from chin to shin,
   she walked and twirled the bottom
   like a shoelace to her car.
To gawk behind a naked
   girl's behind in St. Tropez
   is not unusual.
                  In fact,
   it's almost trite.
                  But this
   was different.
                  Her walking asked
   what form's more beautiful
   in all of nature than the female
   body in its prime?
                  It spoke
   like modern Paris architecture,
   giving not a damn for my approval
   or dissent, but being absolutely
   what it is, take it or leave it . . .
Secure within the purpose
   of herself, she scarcely noticed me.
Of, if she did, she relegated me
   to that dull tribe who wear,
   like public transportation passengers,
   the same church-face
   from breath to death.

                    Her face
was every oiled inch of her
from eyebrows beachward
to her toes.
                    All this she bared
as shamelessly as any wife
undressing as her husband watched.
It woke me up.
                    The south
of France became the Côte
d'Azur.
                    The beach was not
a shore of stones but suddenly
the Riviera.
                    The sky
demanded to be memorized.
The wind remembered it should be
the wind, and every breath
it billowed softly from the sea
was mine to swallow like a song.

The Concise Wisdom of Luggage

Its hide can't hide the earned
  wounds of the road: a dinge
  from Mexico, Bulgarian chalk
  marks, the sun-scents
  of Cannes, and half-peeled
  stamps that spell Swiss-
  Luft-Pan-Air.
                    Storing
  my counted shirts and shorts,
  it waits like a good dog
  for me to claim it.
                    And I do . . .
At first its leathers smelled
  like a new car.
                    Its buff
  interiors recalled aromas
  of shirts being ironed.
                    Now
  it has the flexibility of gloves
  or shoes or pillows I have trained.
It churches me with measure: "Too
  much is too much, but more
  is never enough."
                    Two coasts
  from where I checked it in,
  it ties me to my work,
  my country, and my home.
                    It goes
  where I go.

　　　　　　It stays when
I stay.
　　　　　　Touching it, I touch
whatever it remembers, and I listen
as I listen to Sibelius alone.
For what?
　　　　　　For echoes of that afternoon
in Rome, that evening in Beirut
before the massacres, that flight
to Dublin from the south of France?
It says it's irreplaceable
though it and everything it holds
are totally replaceable.
　　　　　　　　Frankly,
what make it irreplaceable
but me?
　　　　　Losing it, I'd feel
deprived, revengeful, less myself . . .
Because it's home to no one
else but me, I lock it
like a house and keep the key.

JUST ONCE IN ALL MY LIFE

A Toast for the Likes of Two

Who was it wrote, "If women
   had mustaches, they would somehow
   make them beautiful.
                    Look
what they've done with breasts!"
Who disagrees?
                Doesn't the Bible
say a woman just an inch
from death will keep an eye
for color?
           And don't philosophers
agree that women sacrifice
the ultimate on beauty's altar?
And love's . . .
            Why scoff at that?
Are the male gods of money,
   fame, and power more deserving?
What's money but guilt?
              What's fame
but knowing people you will never
know will know your name?
What's power but pride translated
   into force?
           Are these worth more
than what sustains us to the end?
Consider Bertha.
          Eighty, blind,
and diabetic, she believed that death's
real name was Harold.

     "I want
to know what Harold has to offer,"
she would say.
     She'd seen
her children's children's children
and presumed she had a poet's right
to give a name to death, if so
she chose.
     Chuckling to herself,
she rocked and waited for this last
adventure in her life . . .
       Then
there was Jane, who mothered seven
and left unfinished all her art
by choice as if to prove
that incompleteness is the rule
of life where nothing ends
the way it should . . . or when.
Two weeks before her funeral
she called all seven to her bed
to say, "I hope to see you all
again . . . but not right away . . ."
So here's to the honor of Bertha,
and here's to the glory of Jane!
Let them be spoken of wherever
beauty's lovers gather to applaud
the beauty of love.
     Let them
not rest in peace but thrive
in everlasting action, doing
what they love the most.
     Who wants
a heaven that's equivalent to one
long sleep?

Those crypted, supine
saints in their basilicas can keep
the dream of their Jerusalem.
                                        The soul
was meant for more than that.
Pray for us, Saint Bertha.
Pray for us, Saint Jane.

Everything's Important, Everything's Brief

The stroke had killed his English.
All that remained was Swedish
   he no longer spoke because
   the stroke had stilled his tongue
   as well.
          Phoning in his stead
was Monica, who asked if I
would like to hear "the voice
of Tomas."
         A man's voice,
groping for syllables in Swedish
but a man's voice still,
wobbled over the Atlantic
to Pittsburgh from Våsteras.
              Then,
   perfect and lucid as reveille,
   he played a prelude by Chopin.
Because the stroke had spared
   his limbs, his fingers spoke
   to me for three full minutes
   in Chopin.
         Each note was true
and Baltic as the language in his finest
poems . . .
         Afterwards, a pause,
followed by blind laughter
in Swedish, then goodbye.
I sat there, phone in hand,
  re-hearing what I'd hear just once
   in all my life.

                He
made me feel . . .
                        How can I
say this?
                Imagine something
free and beautiful and captive
all at once—like a finger suddenly
enhanced but still imprisoned by a ring.
Like mercy.
                Like a love so unexpected
that it never left its name.

Max

"For Buonarroti," muttered Max
     while triggering the saw's teeth
     through stone, "nothing but two
     hands for this—*tutto a mano.*"
Goggled but otherwise a chalk
     ghost powdered with stone dust,
     he laid his power saw aside
     and stroked it like a tired dog.
After he propped his goggles
     on his head, we sat and smoked.
The stone kept waiting,
          listening, resting.
                         Max showed me
     where the stone was layered—okay
     for fountains, not figures.
                              Fingers
     carved from anything but marble
     from Carrara certainly would crack . . .
Later he washed the bulging
     stone the way a nurse might swab
     the belly of a pregnant woman
     in her bath.
                    In mid-caress
     he stopped as if he touched by chance
     the tick of life within . . .
His face reminded me of Pavarotti's
     in his youth, smaller but more
     refined, less pagan in the jaw.
His eyes hid visions never
     to be known, revisions to be shown

to no one, decisions to be made
in stone or not at all.
                        That's how
   it is with artists who are genuine.
They do what they can't say,
   then speak in pauses or in looks.
Each time I watch them work,
   the world becomes a resurrection.
It brings me back to what I am.
For forty years I've shared
   the living words of buried
   men and women with the young.
I've watched these words do all
   the work like sawteeth biting
   into stone.
                     Today and every day
I'm at it still.
                     Pocketing
my glasses, wiping the chalk-dust
from my palms, I work alone
like any midwife busy with a birth
of words—a laborer—a Max.

                    For Massimiliano Squillace

The Thrower and the Keeper

I claim the Iroquois were right—
   "Travel light, travel far."
                           You say
   the things you chuck today
   you just might need tomorrow.
So here we are—the chucker
   and the saver, now against
   mañana.
             On trips you pack
   for three eventualities—delay,
   disaster, and demise.
                  I pack
   the clothes I plan to leave
   behind, the socks I'll never
   wear at home, the books
   I bring to give away . . .
                To be exact,
   you're two-thirds right.
                 When I
   need dimes for tolls or parking
   meters, presto! you produce
   them from the pocket of your coat.
If I need dollars, presto! out
   they pop like Kleenex from the selfsame
   coat.
         And that trick works
   with any coat.
             You keep
   a history of birthdays, wedding
   dates, and anniversaries, and twice

that saved us from the queen
of all embarrassments.
                          You store
for years the sales receipts
I'd throw away, and once
that spared us a calamity.
                          I doubt
we'll change.
                   What leaves me edgy
makes you more assured, so why
adjust?
          I'll keep on lightening
our overload of blankets, towels,
issues of the *National Geographic*,
Christmas ribbons, water
glasses from a dozen different
sets, galoshes, photographs,
and stubs, discarding, I concede,
some quality in all that quantity.
You'll go on saving snapshots,
   rubber bands, old programs
   from Toronto and New York,
   canceled stamps from Italy
   or Belgium, shillings, francs,
   a ring too tarnished to be worn,
   door keys for God knows which
   hotels, outdated medicines,
   and finally, I gratefully admit,
   some quality in all that quantity,
   including, in the process, me.

To Breathe, to Speak, to Be

A photograph not three years old
   you called "the lie of an earlier
   me."
        Or once when told
about a girl who kept repeating
in her choice of men an old
mistake, you said, "More
the fool she." -
          By heritage
or inspiration, you converse like Shaw
in Shakespearian rhythms.
             Don't
blush.
      It happens differently
the same in different nationalities.
Savoring a poem by Celaya,
   Margarita said in tears, "This
   happinesses me."
          Your way
or hers, it's how our language
welcomes liberties and comes out
richer, truer, fresher.
Each time we turn into our words
   we interrupt what wears us down
   as steadily as bars of soap
   are worn and smoothed away
   like pebbles from the sea.
            The vanity
of victory we put aside.
We shun occasions that transform

a face from innocent to gnarled
more quickly than a hand
becomes a fist.
                    Instead
we see that life and words
are interchangeable and indivisible
as love and genuine contrition.
If anyone proclaims we live
    and die between parentheses,
    we say we really die and live
    between quotation marks.
Important as they are, the years
    are not the ultimate.
                    What's
    crucial is the punctuation.

The First Sam Hazo at the Last

A minor brush with medicine
   in eighty years was all
   he'd known.
                 But this was different.
His right arm limp and slung,
   his right leg dead to feeling
   and response, he let me spoon him
   chicken-broth.
              Later he said
without self-pity that he'd like
   to die.
          I bluffed, "The doctors
think that therapy might help you
walk again."
             "They're liars,
all of them," he muttered.
                   Bedfast
was never how he hoped to go.
"In bed you think of everything,"
   he whispered with a shrug, "you think
   of all of your life."
             I knew
he meant my mother.
              Without her
he was never what he might have been,
and everyone who loved him knew it.
Nothing could take her place—
   not the cars he loved to drive,
   not the money he could earn at will,
   not the roads he knew by heart

from Florida to Saranac, not the two
replacement wives who never
measured up.
                    Fed now by family
or strangers, carried to the john,
shaved and changed by hired help,
this independent man turned silent
at the end.
                    Only my wife
could reach him for his private needs.
What no one else could do
for him, he let her do.
She talked to him and held
    his hand, the left.
                    She helped him
bless himself and prayed beside him
as my mother might have done.
"Darling" was his final word
    for her.
                    Softly, in Arabic.

Reaching for Australia

What is the opposite of two?
A lonely me, a lonely you.

— Richard Wilbur

Remember Epcot?
                    A firing
    squad of clocks took aim
    at us from jade mountains,
    the golden bellies of Buddhas,
    ships' hulls, painted
    waterfalls, and other settings
    only China could devise.
                            Three
    centuries away from quartz
    and digital, they marched in step—
    one tortoise-tick for each
    twelfth-tock of the hare.
Under the razzamatazz and schlock
    the core of every timepiece
    chimed and rhymed with zero.
I thought of suns or eyes
    of hurricanes or anything
    that spins all else around it
    into life.
                Like a wheel's
hub.
        Like the stone that's key
    in every Roman arch.
                            That stone
    puts all the other stones
    to work by being where and what

it is, and that's enough.
Each arch-half strains against
    its opposite like shorelines
    shaping rivers as they flow—
    like women hugging men
    they love against their bellies
    with their thighs.
                        At times
    like that, life matters more
    than being clocked and numbered
    down to dust . . .
                        Each time we talk
    by phone we prove the clocks
    of loving have no hands.
I know that land-miles
    and the whole Pacific separate us.
According to the almanac, you're
    halfway through an afternoon
    I've yet to reach.
                        Unparted
    but apart, we see so much
    deployed against and in between
    the tiny unity of us.
                        But then,
    just then, our voices reach around
    the world—like arms—and touch.

The Last Shall Be First and Only

If anybody speaks their names,
   I still recall them as they were—
   approachable, intelligent, attractive,
   and single.
          Shirley, dead
   at fifty; Janet, who married
   badly; Yvonne, grandmotherly
   in Georgia; Rose Anita,
   whereabouts unknown, and Susie,
   whereabouts unknowable . . .
                Each pairing
   at the time seemed right until—
Today like photos in a yearbook
   they present as real the dream
   I call the past.
          What
   does it prove?
          Looking for love
   in the wrong season, never
   finding it, then not looking
   and being found by it . . .
Despite a million variations
   that's the formula.
          The rest
   is choice and work and mystery
   and luck, much luck.
          Power's
   a poor replacement.
          Money's
   poorer, and casual philandering's

the poorest of them all.
My wife's
my understander.
In matters of romance
she outranks me in wisdom
as a queen outranks a rook.
Like Siamese twins we're fused
at head, hip, and heart.
I hurt
when she hurts, hate anyone
who disconcerts her, mope
if I miss, as I have, a birthday,
and, in short, seem out of sorts
when she's away for long.
We wonder who will die the first.
"If I should linger, promise
me a view where I can see
the flowers."
"Since words are where
I live, just keep the coffin
closed and stand my books on top."
No matter where we are, we stay
in touch by telephone or mail
to say what keeps two souls
together though alone, alone
together.
On trivia we disagree
but still defend good Democrats,
eat mussels from the selfsame dish,
are bored by monologues from chatterers,
and trust a carpenter named Christ
to figure out our praying . . .
That's not
quite all, but so far that's enough.

Ballad of the Old Lovers

"Your body's slowed down, my dearest dear.
Your body's slowed down, my dearest."
"I'm aging, my dear—just aging, I fear.
Each day I keep growing older . . .
The birds in the trees may never freeze,
but the blood as you age grows colder."

"Remember the days when we used to play
and hug on the sheets of the bed there?
You'd touch me here and touch me here,
and then we would wrestle together?
Instead we lie now like the dead there
and listen all night to the weather."

"Remember the money we managed to save
and planned to enjoy in our sixties?
Well, sixty has come, and sixty has gone,
and what have our savings returned us
but travel in season without a good reason
and tropical sunlight that burned us?"

"Remember the friends we knew, we knew,
when we and our friends were younger?
Where have they gone, and why don't they write,
and why have the decades divided
all those not alive from those who survive
no matter how well they're provided?"

"But why blame our fears on the innocent years?
They're gone and beyond re-living.

Since death's quite efficient, and time's insufficient,
is it asking too much to forgive us
for wanting to stay till the end of the day
and love what the years can still give us?"

"So give me a kiss, my dearest of dears,
and sleep by my side forever.
Let the years come, and let the years go.
We treasure what nothing can sever.
In touch or apart is the same to the heart.
Until death parts us not, we're together."

NO FUTURE BUT
THE TIME AT HAND

Dead End

The road just stopped where woods
   began as if it somehow
   lost its purpose.
                  Like lives
too numerous to list, it died
abruptly in full stride,
headed for highways it would
never reach.
                  Straight as a bandage
through the fields or looping
like a lasso up a mountainside,
its past was visible for miles.
It kept what all roads keep—
   a deep imperative of motion,
   beckoning the traveler in all of us
   to dream of destinations . . .
                  What made
   the builders quit?
                  Lack
of cash or property disputes?
Or was it to remind inquisitors
   like me that there are finishes
   beyond anticipation?
                  Lethal
as lightning and as quick, they strike
when they are least expected.
They contradict.
                  They scrap our maps.
They say some destinations are

the ones we're heading for, but some
are not.
      Like roads that go
so far but not a breath farther . . .

For Gregor Meyer

American Pastoral

Nothing spectacular about the day—
   three clouds of no distinction
   and a sky as blue as a clear,
   unrippled bay.
           To the left,
   a silo painted red, a slant-roofed
   barn the color of copper,
   and a gray house with green shutters
   cramped between willows.
                 No more
   than that unless you count
   a two-track driveway ramming
   a gravel road that no one
   but the farmer uses . . .
             Easy
   to romanticize the place, but I
   demur.
        I've worked a farm.
I know the sweat it takes.
And down the years I've seen
   so many farms like this,
   so many.
          What strikes me now
   is how a scene so undisturbed
   and typical beneath an absolutely
   undramatic sky could somehow be
   this true, this rare, this unforgettable.

A Time of No Shadows

Immortality?
                 Too general a concept.
Some say it's never-ending time,
    which means it's long on myth
    but short on meaning.
                      Some say
    it's never to be known until
    it's ours.
                   Some say, some say . . .
I stand with those who think
    it could be quick as any instant
    going on and on and on
    within itself like poetry or music
    or a kiss.
                 That comes as close
    as anything to God's "*I am
    Who am.*"
                 No past.
                           No memory.
No future but the time at hand
    that's passing even as it's born . . .
Once I was driving due southeast
    through Pennsylvania.
                          Highways
    were broad and dangerous and everyone's.
As I ran out of Pennsylvania,
    farm by farm, I noticed
    border signs that welcomed me
    to Maryland where Rand McNally
    said that Maryland began.

I knew the earth was still
   the earth in Maryland or Pennsylvania.
I knew I stayed the same,
    border or no border . . .
                  From here
into hereafter could be just
like that—our selfsame selves
translated instantly from state
to state to God alone
knows what . . .
               That's immortality.

Where After This?

Is it enough to be disgusted
   with the age?
             The same hitlers
reappear with different names,
and half the nations of the world
are ruled by some ex-murderer
or worse.
          Right now a prisoner
in solitary somewhere screams
for his wife.
           It's been five years.
Is it enough to mention this
   and let it go?
            The Greeks believe
"injustice is a wound that never
sleeps."
         And everywhere that's so.
But what's the cure?
             Perpetual
rebellion, vengeance, redress,
or simply knowing wrong
from right and standing up
and saying so?
          If evil still prevails,
at least we never were accomplices.
In Southeast Asia once
   we said we killed to cure,
   bombing villages to save them,
Vietnamizing the Vietnamese.

                                        All this
    for what is now regarded
    as a serious mistake by those
    in power then who ordered it.
Like ancient mariners they tour
    the world, confessing even
    to their enemies and hoping to be
    understood, redeemed, forgiven.
If life means living on with wounds,
    they live as best they can.
                            Under
    the scabs the wounds still bleed.

Arms and the Word

Great sailors though they were,
   the Greeks abhorred the sea.
What was it but a gray
   monotony of waves, wetness
   in depth, an element by nature
   voyager-unfriendly and capricious?
Sailing in sight of shore,
   they always beached at night
   to sleep before the next day's
   rowing.
          Taming the sea
   by beating it with rods
   they named the ultimate insanity—
   a metaphor too obvious to paraphrase.
In short, they knew a widow-
   maker when they saw one.
                 Still,
   for honor, commerce, or a kidnaped
   queen, they waged their lives
   against what Homer called wine-dark
   and deep.
          Some came back never.
Some learned too late that pacing
   a deck was far less hazardous
   than facing what awaited them
   at home . . .
          Homer would praise
   their iliads and odysseys in song.
Aeschylus, Euripides, and Sophocles
   would watch and wait, then write

of wars much closer to the heart.
They knew the lives of men—
    no matter how adventurous—
    would end as comedies or tragedies.
They wrote that both were fundamentally
    and finally domestic.
                    Homer
    could sing his fill.
                    The dramatists
    dared otherwise.
                    Compared
    to troubles in a family, they saw
    this business with the sea and swords—
    regardless of the risk—as temporary.

Where Were You When?

Training for trouble is a waste
    of time.
               It makes you think
    of generals preparing armies
    daily for the last war.
When sellers of insurance
    calculate a policy that covers you
    against explosions, loss
    of fingers, flooding, sleeping
    sickness, lightning, rattlesnakes,
    or ricochets, you say you're only
    hoping for a good death,
    regardless of the cause.
                  They tell you
    no insurance can assure you that . . .
Troubles ago, you ran uphill
    and walked downhill.
                 Today
    you realize that you were strengthening
    yourself against the unevadable . . .
You do it still, but now
    your hills are poems you attempt
    to finish, rumors of war,
    or policies hatched by fools.
Like anyone confronted by the once
    of anything, you try your best
    to be significant.
              If nothing works,
    at least you tried.

When critics
stone you with their looks
or words, you know that most
attempters fared no better . . .
Why waste your prowess on defense?
Salvation's not a matter
of deterrence by the wise and well
prepared.
It's how you think
and what you do when something
unavoidable confronts you all
at once.
It's always a surprise.

Ahead of Time

Her letter, mailed from Saranac,
   is dated 1926.
                  My mother's
writing to my aunt.
                  It's two
years since she told her father,
"Dad, I'm marrying Sam
and not the man you had
in mind."
              That's decades more
   than half a century ago.
My mother and my aunt are dead.
I'm well past sixty when I share
   my mother's letter with my wife.
It stills us like a resurrection.
Later I read it to my son
   and to his wife.
                  They tell me
how alive it seems as if
a woman neither ever knew
is speaking in this very room
to each of us.
                  The letter's full
of questions I can answer,
but the time for answering is over.
I realize my life's already longer
   than my mother's was by almost
   thirty years.
                  The letter in my hand
   is older than the two of us.

The more I read, the less
   there is to read until
   I reach the bottom of the page.
The last sentence ends
   with a hyphen.
                    There's no page two.